ZOMBIE ANIMALS
PARASITES TAKE CONTROL!

ZOMBIE GRASSHOPPERS

BY JOLENE ALESSI

Gareth Stevens
PUBLISHING

Please visit our website, www.garethstevens.com. For a free color catalog of all our high-quality books, call toll free 1-800-542-2595 or fax 1-877-542-2596.

Library of Congress Cataloging-in-Publication Data

Alessi, Jolene, author.
 Zombie grasshoppers / Jolene Alessi.
     pages cm. — (Zombie animals: Parasites take control!)
 Includes bibliographical references and index.
 ISBN 978-1-4824-2844-5 (pbk.)
 ISBN 978-1-4824-2845-2 (6 pack)
 ISBN 978-1-4824-2846-9 (library binding)
 1. Parasites—Juvenile literature. 2. Grasshoppers—Parasites—Juvenile literature. I. Title. II. Series: Zombie animals. Parasites take control!
 QL757.A663 2015
 595.7'26—dc23
                                                                                                         2015006981

First Edition

Published in 2016 by
Gareth Stevens Publishing
111 East 14th Street, Suite 349
New York, NY 10003

Copyright © 2016 Gareth Stevens Publishing

Designer: Samantha DeMartin
Editor: Kristen Rajczak

Photo credits: Cover, p. 1 Sarah2/Shutterstock.com; p. 5 Brian Maudsley/Shutterstock.com; p. 7 Photo Researchers/Science Source/Getty Images; p. 9 Vitalii Hulai/Shutterstock.com; p. 11 hakuna_jina/Shutterstock.com; p. 13 evantravels/Shutterstock.com; p. 15, 21 (grasshopper by water) Vladmir Kim/Shutterstock.com; p. 17, 21 (grasshopper with hairworm) Dr. Andreas Schmidt-Rhaesa/Wikimedia Commons; p. 19 Alastair Rae/Wikimedia Commons; p. 20 Nikita Starichenko/Shutterstock.com.

Printed in the United States of America

CPSIA compliance information: Batch #CS15GS: For further information contact Gareth Stevens, New York, New York at 1-800-542-2595.

CONTENTS

Words in the glossary appear in **bold** type the first time they are used in the text.

FORCED TO JUMP

Do you know how to swim? Imagine that you don't, and someone made you jump into the water without anything to help you float. That's what happens to grasshoppers that are **infected** by a parasite called a hairworm.

While you'd probably be scared and angry about being made to jump, a parasite-infected grasshopper doesn't make a fuss about it. The hairworm is in complete control of it. The grasshopper is nothing more than a zombie!

TAKE-OVER TRUTHS

A PARASITE IS AN **ORGANISM** THAT LIVES ON OR IN ANOTHER ORGANISM, CALLED A HOST. PARASITES OFTEN CAUSE THEIR HOST HARM.

Grasshoppers are commonly bugs that fly—not swim!

HORRIBLE HAIRWORM

Hairworms are parasites that belong to the animal group Nematomorpha. There are 350 species, or kinds of organisms, in Nematomorpha. The species that infects grasshoppers is called *S. tellinii*. Other bugs face a total take-over from this hairworm, too. Katydids and crickets are also hosts for *S. tellinii*!

Hairworms are only parasites for part of their life. They use their hosts to grow into adults. As adults, hairworms look like thick pieces of string. They can be as long as 3.3 feet (1 m)!

TAKE-OVER TRUTHS

THERE ARE TWO KINDS OF ORGANISMS IN NEMATOMORPHA. ONE GROUP INFECTS **ARTHROPODS** THAT LIVE ON LAND. THE OTHER INFECTS MARINE, OR SEA, ARTHROPODS LIKE SHRIMP AND CRABS.

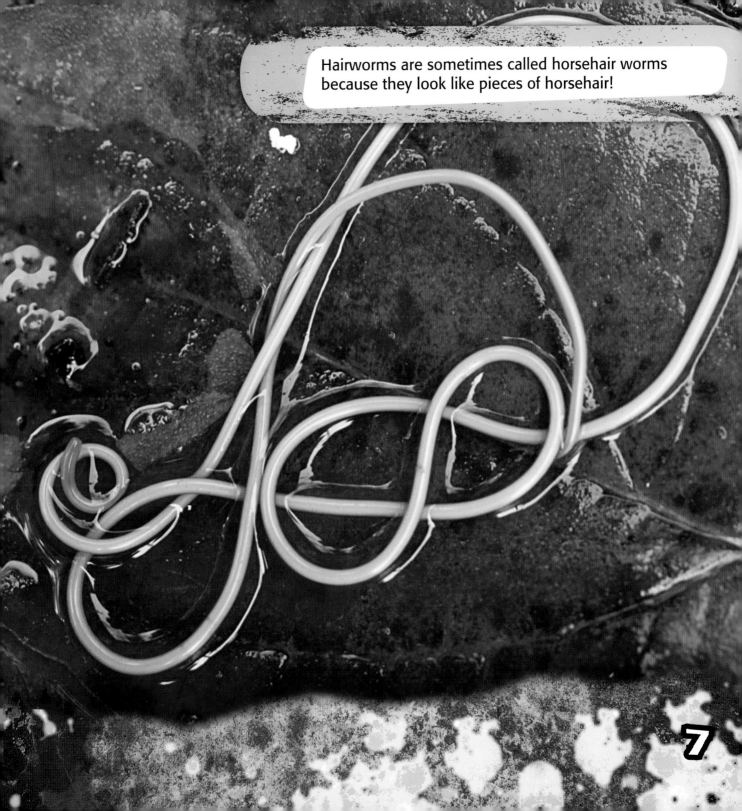

TRANSPORT HOST

Hairworms live and **breed** in freshwater. A hairworm lays as many as 10 million eggs in lakes, rivers, and streams. When their larvae hatch, they stay near the bottom of a body of water, hoping to be eaten. Each larva is looking for a transport host, or an organism such as an insect that will get it to its final host—the grasshopper.

The larva makes a **cyst** around itself when inside the transport host. If it's lucky, a grasshopper eats the transport host.

TAKE-OVER TRUTHS

HAIRWORMS HAVE BEEN FOUND ON EVERY CONTINENT EXCEPT ANTARCTICA.

Often, the transport host—like this snail—is a dead end for a hairworm larva because the host isn't food for the grasshopper, cricket, or katydid it wants to find.

GRASSHOPPER FOR LUNCH

Once a grasshopper eats a hairworm larva, the larva can feast! Inside the grasshopper, the larva will **develop** into an adult hairworm. To do that, it needs to eat a lot. The growing hairworm eats every part of the grasshopper's insides it can while still keeping the grasshopper alive.

The hairworm grows so large that it fills most of the grasshopper's body in time. If laid out end-to-end, adult hairworms are about three to four times longer than their hosts.

TAKE-OVER TRUTHS

SOME SCIENTISTS BELIEVE IT'S POSSIBLE FOR SOME GRASSHOPPERS TO BECOME INFECTED WITH A HAIRWORM BY DRINKING WATER WITH LARVAE IN IT.

The hairworm needs its grasshopper host alive so it can reach the next part of its life cycle.

INFECTED!

Throughout the hairworm's growth, the grasshopper doesn't fight back. It likely doesn't know it's been infected! The hairworm growing inside it has taken over the grasshopper's **nervous system**, which includes the brain.

The hairworm produces **proteins** that **mimic** those created by the grasshopper's nervous system. These proteins begin to tell the brain to do what the parasite wants—and the grasshopper becomes a zombie! In addition, scientists have found that infected grasshoppers produce different brain proteins than uninfected grasshoppers.

TAKE-OVER TRUTHS

IN RECENT YEARS, THERE HAS BEEN A LOT OF STUDY ON HOSTS THAT ARE ZOMBIFIED. THERE'S STILL A LOT SCIENTISTS DON'T KNOW ABOUT HOW THIS HAPPENS!

For a long time, scientists weren't sure if parasites like *S. tellinii* were controlling their hosts on purpose. Now, it's believed they are!

LOOKING FOR WATER

S. tellinii has a good reason to make the grasshopper a zombie. It wants the grasshopper to take it back to the water where it can **reproduce**. However, grasshoppers don't normally live on or in water. The hairworm uses its control of the grasshopper to force it to head toward water.

Picture a pond. The sun is shining and birds are chirping. But down at the edge, a grasshopper—which can't swim—is being forced to dive into the water to its death!

While hairworms will force grasshoppers toward water, they won't push them to travel a great distance to reach it.

THE HAIRWORM LIVES ON

Once the grasshopper's body is in the water, the adult hairworm can begin its free-swimming life in the water. The hairworm leaves the grasshopper through its rear end and swims off to find a **mate**. Without the zombie grasshopper, a hairworm wouldn't be able to complete its life cycle!

Scientists have found that the presence of parasites in nature is a sign of health. If you happen to see a grasshopper leaping to its death, you'll know that area is doing just fine!

TAKE-OVER TRUTHS

VERY FEW PARASITES IN THE WORLD CAN MAKE HOSTS INTO ZOMBIES.

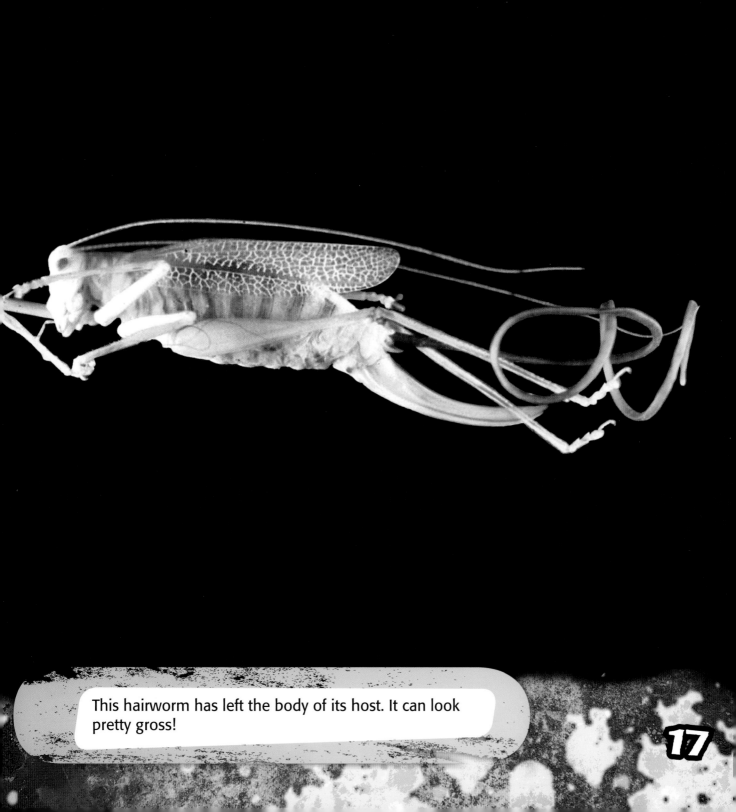

This hairworm has left the body of its host. It can look pretty gross!

HOW DO WE KNOW?

Much of what we know about zombie grasshoppers and the hairworm comes from a group of French **biologists**. They observed hundreds of infected grasshoppers who, under the control of parasites, were headed toward a swimming pool near a forest. Before the grasshoppers could take the leap of death, the biologists caught them.

Then, they took the worms out of the grasshoppers and studied them. It was these biologists who discovered the hairworms' proteins mimicked those of the grasshoppers.

This adult hairworm grew large inside its host, a cricket. Its size makes it easy for scientists to study.

MORE PARASITES

S. tellinii is just one parasite that infects grasshoppers. Insects belonging to the group Scelionidae ride on female grasshoppers until the grasshoppers lay their eggs. Then, the scelionids attack the eggs! Another kind of fly lays eggs inside a grasshopper, where they hatch into larvae and grow.

These parasites might cause their grasshopper hosts harm. Some grasshoppers might even die because of the parasite. However, the hairworm seems to be the only grasshopper parasite that can turn its host into a zombie!

TAKE-OVER TRUTHS

SOMETIMES PARASITES ARE USED TO CONTROL POPULATIONS OF GRASSHOPPERS THAT ARE HARMING FARMERS' CROPS!

LIFE CYCLE OF THE HAIRWORM

hairworm breeds and lays eggs

hairworm larva hatches

larva is eaten by a transport host

grasshopper eats transport host

larva develops into an adult and takes over the grasshopper

grasshopper is forced to jump into water and dies

hairworm leaves the grasshopper's body

GLOSSARY

arthropod: an animal that lacks a backbone and has a skeleton on the outside of its body, such as an insect, spider, shrimp, or crab

biologist: a scientist who studies life on Earth

breed: to come together to make babies

cyst: a sac that surrounds and protects an organism in its larva stage

develop: to grow and change

infect: to spread something harmful inside the body

mate: one of two animals that come together to produce babies

mimic: to copy

nervous system: the body system that includes the brain, spinal cord, and other body parts that send and receive messages throughout the body

organism: a living thing

protein: matter created by the body that carries out different jobs inside the body

reproduce: when an animal creates another creature just like itself

FOR MORE INFORMATION

BOOKS

Larson, Kirsten. *Zombies in Nature*. Mankato, MN: Amicus, 2016.

Spilsbury, Richard. *Zoom in on Bizarre Bugs*. Berkeley Heights, NJ: Enslow Publishers, 2013.

Trueit, Trudi Strain. *Grasshoppers*. New York, NY: Marshall Cavendish, 2013.

WEBSITES

Grasshoppers
www.biokids.umich.edu/critters/Acrididae/
Learn more about grasshoppers that *haven't* become zombies!

So, You Want a Pet Parasite?
discoverykids.com/games/so-you-want-a-pet-parasite/
Play this fun game to learn about more parasites.

INDEX